You Laugh You Lose Challenge

Challenge

300 Jokes for Kids That Are Funny, Silly, And Interactive Fun the Whole Family Will Love

11-Year-Old Edition

You Laugh You Lose Series Volume 6

~With Illustrations for Kids~

Smiley Beagle

Copyright © 2020 by Sea Vision Publishing, LLC

All Rights Reserved.

No part of this publication may be reproduced, distributed, or transmitted in any form or by any means, including photocopying, recording, electronic or mechanical methods, without the prior written permission of the publisher, except in the case of brief quotations embodied in critical reviews and certain other non-commercial uses permitted by copyright law.

ISBN: 9798666706046

Table of Contents

Introduction

We know you are getting older, and so is your taste in jokes! We know you feel like you have heard them all, but we think we may have a joke or two left up our sleeve to surprise you. Check our whole new book of jokes meant for the kids who are growing up. You are maturing every day and want more mature jokes, and we get it. Though, we may have hidden a goofy one or two in there.

These are jokes that we searched high and low for, just to make sure that only the funniest funnies and most hilarious puns got in. We are picky jokesters, and we know our readers have a refined sense of humor. But even if you don't, we still want to make you laugh.

We are excited to grow older, and we want your journey to always be filled with laughter and good times.

Rules

Each player takes a turn reading one joke from the book. If somebody laughs, then the person reading it gets a point. The book is then given to the next player, and it is their turn to read.

Smiling at the joke doesn't count, but any sort of laughing is worth 1 point. The first person to reach 7 points wins! Feel free to play with as many people as you want or even form teams to make funny faces to try and get everyone in on the laughing.

Remember to be fair and always admit if you laugh, games with arguments are no fun. And the most important thing of all is to laugh as much as you can!

Going Solo

Want to try to beat the "You Laugh You Lose" challenge on your own? Think you got what it takes to beat one of the funniest books around? Want to brag to your friends!

See how far you can get without cracking up! When you are done, use the scoring system below to see how well you did.

10 jokes – A Jester, At Best!

25 jokes – The Town Clown!

50 jokes – Passable Prankster!

100 jokes – Chuckle Champion!

150 jokes – Wisecrack Wizard!

200 jokes – Ha-Ha Hero!

300 jokes – Laugh Legend!

Chapter One
Tech Jokes

1. "Doctor, I keep stealing things."

"Take some tablets; if that doesn't work, get me a flat-screen TV."

2. I love pressing F5.

It's so refreshing.

3. Why shouldn't you tell a chemistry joke?

Because the person you tell it to might get a reaction!

4. I've got a phobia of over-engineered buildings.

It's a complex complex complex!

5. My friend made a joke about a TV controller...

It wasn't remotely funny!

6. What did the kid do when his scooter got stolen?

He moped!

7. My fear of moving stairs is escalating!

8. Which way did the computer programmer go?

He went data way!

9. Why did the developer go broke?

Because he used up all his cache!

10. How does a computer finish a sandwich?

Bit by bit!

11. Why did the computer spy quit?

He couldn't hack it anymore!

12. What did the computer do at lunchtime?

It had a byte!

13. How did the computers buy a new car?

They all chipped in!

14. Wanna hear a joke about potassium?

K!

15. Do you know any good jokes about sodium?

Na!

16. What did the paper clip say to the magnet?

"I find you very attractive!"

17. Why can't the elephant use the computer?

Because he's afraid of the mouse!

18. What musical instrument do computers like to play?

The keyboard!

19. What makes cyber-dogs itchy?

Roboticks!

20. What do robots wear under their shorts?

Underware!

Chapter Two
Long Jokes

1. An old married couple is in church one Sunday...

The woman turns to her husband and says, "I've just let out a really long, silent fart. What should I do?"

The husband turns to her and says, "Replace the battery in your hearing aid."

2. A man is walking along, carrying a giraffe under each arm. While not paying attention, he accidentally drops the giraffe. A passerby points it out, annoyed, "Are you going to leave that lying there?"

The man replied, "That's a giraffe, not a lion."

3. A magician calls a boy from the audience on to the stage.

He gives his hand and asks kindly,

"Do you know me, boy? Have you seen me before?"

"No, Dad!"

4. Will you remember me a year from now?

Yes.

Will you remember me tomorrow?

Yes.

Will you remember me when you grow old?

Yes.

Knock, knock...

Who's there?

I thought you said you'd remember me?!?

5. A mother sings a lullaby for her daughter at night.

She sings for an hour, two, three...

She got tired and decided to take a break.

Suddenly the daughter opens her eyes and asks, "Mom, are you done? I want to go to sleep."

6. A small boy swallowed some coins and was taken to the hospital.

When his grandmother called the doctor to ask how he was doing, he said, "No change yet."

7. Farmers earn a meager celery, come home beet, and just want to read the pepper, turn-ip the covers, en-dive into bed!

8. A dog walks into a job center. "Wow, a talking dog," says the clerk. "With your talent, I'm sure we can find you a gig in the circus."

"The circus?" says the dog. "What does a circus want with a plumber?"

9. Daphne: "I was born in New York City."

Val: "Which part?"

Daphne: "All of me."

10. Daphne: "I found four horseshoes today."

Val: "Do you know what that means?"

Daphne: "There is a barefoot horse running somewhere."

11. Daphne: "I saw a huge car in the street. It was like a house."

Val: "Why are you exaggerating? I told you a hundred million times that this is a bad habit!"

12. Doctor it hurts when I touch here (touches face), and here (touches arm), and here (touches chest) ...

The doctor takes a look at him and says, "You have a broken finger."

13. A church's bell ringer passes away, so they post the position.

A man with no arms comes in to apply for the job.

The clergy isn't sure he can do it, but he convinces them to let him try it.

So, they all climb to the top of the bell tower, and the guy runs toward the bell and hits it hard with his head. They give him the job.

The next day, the new bell ringer goes to the bell tower to ring the bell. As he runs into the bell, he trips, bounces off the bell, and falls out the tower onto the sidewalk below.

Two guys are walking past. One asks, "Do you know this guy?"

The second guy replies, "No, but his face rings a bell."

14. The next day, the dead bell ringer's twin brother comes in for the again vacant bell ringer position and is hired on the spot.

The next day, when he goes to ring the bell, he, too, trips and falls from the bell tower onto the sidewalk below.

The same two guys walk by.

The first asks, "Do you know who that is?"

The second guy responds, "No, but he's a dead ringer for his brother."

15. Two guys are camping when they see a bear.

One guy sprints back to the tent and trades his hiking boots for a pair on running shoes.

His friend, seeing what he is doing, asks, "What are you doing? You can't outrun a bear!"

He says, "I don't have to outrun the bear. I have to outrun you!"

16. Sherlock Holmes and Dr. Watson went camping.

They pitched their tent under the stars and went to sleep.

Sometime in the middle of the night, Holmes woke Watson up and said, "Watson, look up at the stars, and tell me what you see."

Watson replied, "I see millions and millions of stars."

Holmes said, "And what do you deduce from that?"

Watson replied, "Well, if there are millions of stars, and if even a few of those have planets, it's quite likely there are some planets like Earth out there. And if there are a few planets like Earth out there, there might also be life."

And Holmes said, "Watson, you idiot, it means that somebody stole our tent."

Chapter Three
Animal Jokes

1. What would a bear say if he got confused?

I barely understand!

2. Why couldn't the leopard play hide and seek?

Because he was always spotted!

3. Why do dragons sleep during the day?

So they can fight knights!

4. Have you ever seen an elephant hiding in a jar of jelly beans?

They hide pretty good, don't they!

5. What kind of fox works for the Red Cross?

A first-aid Kit!

6. How does a lion greet the other animals in the field?

Pleased to eat you!

7. What is it called when you borrow money to buy a bison?

A buffaloan!

8. What did one pig say to the other?

Let's be pen pals!

9. Why do cows lie down when it's cold?

To keep each udder warm!

10. Why are anteaters good workers?

Because a little aardvark never hurt anyone!

11. Why did the chicken walk on the telephone wire?

She wanted to lay it on the line!

12. What is black and white and eats like a horse?

A zebra!

13. Why should you not let a bear operate the remote?

He will keep pressing the paws button!

14. When will the little snake arrive?

I don't know, but he won't be long!

15. How do you shoot a killer bee?

With a bee-bee gun!

16. Who lost a herd of elephants?

Big bo-peep!

17. When do monkeys fall from the sky?

During APE-ril showers!

18. What do you call a pig thief?

A ham burglar!

19. How can a leopard change his spots?

By moving!

20. What do you call a dinosaur wizard?

A dino sorcerer!

21. What do you call two octopuses that look exactly the same?

Itenticle!

22. What do you call a dead parrot?

Polygon!

23. What do you call a pessimistic toucan?

A toucan't!

24. What do you call a baby monkey?

A chimp off the old block!

25. Why do ambassadors never get sick?

Diplomatic immunity!

26. What is a chicken crossing the road?

Poultry in motion!

27. How many bugs do you need to rent out an apartment?

Tenants!

28. What do you use to make hyena soup?

Laughing stock!

29. What does my dog do when he goes to bed?

He reads a bite-time story!

30. Why do male deers need braces?

Because they have buck teeth!

31. What do you call a crying camel?

A humpback wail!

32. Where did the turtle get a new shell?

From the hard-wear store!

33. Which circus performers can see in the dark?

The acro-bats!

34. Daphne: "I taught my monkey to play chess."

Val: "He must be very smart."

Daphne: "Not really, I beat her two games out of three!"

35. Where do chimps get their gossip?

On the ape vine!

36. What kind of ties do pigs wear?

Pigs-ties!

37. Who makes the best prehistoric reptile clothes?

A dino-sewer!

38. Why do dogs have fur coats?

Because they look silly wearing windbreakers!

39. What do you get if you cross a dog and an airplane?

A jet setter!

40. Outside of a dog, a book is man's best friend.

Inside of a dog, it's too dark to read.

41. What is the difference between a duck with one wing and a duck with two wings?

Why, that's a difference of a pinion!

42. What do you give a sick horse?

Cough stirrup!

43. What sickness do horses hate the most?

Hay fever!

44. What bird is with you at every meal?

A swallow!

45. Why do you get if you cross a chili pepper, a shovel, and a terrier?

A hot-diggity-dog!

46. What kind of dog likes to smell flowers?

A bud hound!

47. Why did the pig become an actor?

Because he was a ham!

48. What does a frog say when it washes a window?

"Rub it, rub it, rub it!"

49. What snakes are good at doing sums?

Adders!

50. What was T. Rex's favorite number?

Eight!

51. What do you get if you cross a grizzly bear and a harp?

A bear-faced lyre!

52. What kind of cats like to go bowling?

Alley cats!

53. What is an insect's favorite sport?

Cricket!

54. What has a spiked tail, plates on its back, and sixteen wheels?

A Stegosaurus on roller skates!

55. What is a frog's favorite game?

Croak-et!

56. Why do you need a license for a dog but not for a cat?

Cats can't drive!

57. Why are owls so famous in the woods?

They're the whose-who of the woods!

58. What is a dog's favorite exercise?

Laps!

59. Where are mosquitoes in winter?

I don't know. But I want them to stay there in the summer too.

60. What is 10 feet tall, has 4 jaws, and 25 pairs of antennas?

I don't know, but let's run!

61. How does a dentist work on a hippo?

From the outside, preferably!

62. What do you call a dog with no hind legs and a metal butt?

Sparky!

63. What's the best way to talk to a T-Rex?

From a distance!

64. What did the duck say to the clown?

You quack me up!

65. Why are tigers terrible storytellers?

Because they only have one tail!

66. Why did the horse chew with his mouth open?

Because he had bad stable manners!

67. Have you heard of the pregnant bed bug?

She's going to have her baby in the spring!

68. Why do two birds in a nest always agree?

'Cos they don't wanna fall out!

69. Why is it cheap to feed giraffes?

Because a little goes a long way!

70. What is it about birthdays that make kangaroos unhappy?

They only get to celebrate them in leap years!

71. Why did the dinosaur refuse to wear deodorant?

He didn't want to be ex-stink!

72. Why do monkeys like to eat bananas?

Because they have appeal!

Chapter Four
People Jokes

1. How do you learn to be a trash collector?

Just pick it up as you go along.

2. What kind of music do chiropractors listen to?

Mostly hip-pop!

3. Why does a captain always go down with his ship?

If he didn't, he'd have to pay for the new one!

4. How did the coward die?

He was scared half to death twice!

5. Who was married to Mr. Ippi?

Mississippi!

6. What do you call a ghost who only haunts the town hall?

The nightmayor!

7. Did you hear about the two burglars that fell into a cement mixer?

Police are looking for two hardened criminals!

8. Why do pirates walk the plank?

Because they don't want dogs on the boat!

9. Man in bookstore: "Where is the Self-Help section, please?"

Saleswoman: "If I told you that, it would defeat the purpose."

10. What happened when the magician got mad?

She pulled her hare out!

11. Why did the girl nibble on her calendar?

She wanted a sundae!

12. A courtroom artist was arrested today for an unknown reason.

Details are sketchy!

13. What do you call a woman who crawls up walls?

Ivy!

14. What did the chef name his son?

Stew!

15. I told my doctor, "It hurts when I do this."

He said, "Don't do that."

16. How do celebrities stay cool?

They have lots of fans!

17. What do you call the death of a guy who is hit by a falling ax?

Axe-i-dental!

18. My teacher told me to have a good day.

So I went home!

19. "If you were to clean a vacuum, would you be a vacuum cleaner?"

20. "I like telling dad jokes."

"Sometimes he laughs."

21. My grandfather has the heart of a lion...

...and a lifetime ban from the zoo!

22. A window washer decided he wasn't going to clean the windows on a tall office building

He was worried he was going to kick the bucket!

23. Where do dentists go on vacation?

Floss Vegas!

24. What is a chimney sweeps' most common ailment?

The flu!

25. What makes a good dental patient?

They know the drill!

26. Why did the relationship end between the dentist and a manicurist?

Because they constantly fought tooth and nail!

27. Why was the photographer sad?

Because he had a photographic memory which was never developed.

28. What did the guitar say to the musician?

Pick on someone your own size!

29. What happens to deposed kings?

They get throne away!

30. What was the average age of a caveman?

Stone Age!

31. What kind of ships do students study on?

Scholarships!

32. Did you hear about the power outage at the mall?

Forty shoppers were stuck on the escalator for three hours!

33. **What is a teacher's favorite country?**

Expla-nation!

34. **Where do chemists like to eat?**

At the periodic table!

35. **What did the cowboy say to the dachshund puppies?**

"Git along, little doggies!"

36. **Why are snakes hard to fool?**

You can't pull their leg!

37. **What new crop did the farmer plant?**

Beets me!

38. Why did the clown wear loud socks?

So his feet wouldn't fall asleep!

39. What material do you use to make a clown outfit?

Poly-jester!

40. Patient: "I think I'm a pair of curtains!"

Doctor: "Pull yourself together!"

41. Patient: "I think I'm a needle!"

Doctor: "Yes, I can see your point!"

42. Why was the musician arrested?

Because she got in treble!

43. What do you call a pirate that skips class?

Captain Hooky!

44. Why didn't the pirate's phone work?

Because he left it off the hook!

45. What are pirates afraid of?

The darrrrk!

46. Why did everyone want the music teacher to be on their baseball team?

Because she had the perfect pitch!

47. Why did the cyclops stop teaching?

Because he only had one pupil!

48. What is a golfer's favorite drink?

Tee!

49. What do you call a man in the mailbox?

Bill!

50. How did the Vikings send secret messages?

By Norse code!

51. What is the Pope's favorite scent?

Pope-pourri!

52. Why was Cinderella bad at soccer?

Because she ran away from the ball!

53. Why was her coach a bad coach?

Because he turned back into a pumpkin!

54. What did the teacher do at the beach?

She tested the water!

55. What did the students do when their shoelaces got tangled together?

They went on a class trip!

56. Patient: "Doctor, I get heartburn every time I eat birthday cake."

Doctor: "Next time, take off the candles."

57. Why did the mom not like buying onesies for her baby?

She had twins!

58. Why did the writer want to be buried in a different cemetery when he died?

He didn't like the plot!

59. Did you hear about the actor who fell through the theater's floor?

He was going through a stage!

Chapter Five
Food Jokes

1. **What do call a mac 'n cheese that gets all up in your face?**

Too close for comfort food!

2. **How does milk introduce itself in Spanish?**

Soy milk!

3. **What do you call a rotten hot dog?**

A rankfurter!

4. I am on a seafood diet.

I see food, and I eat it!

5. What is the hardest part of hunting for food?

Figuring out where sandwiches live!

6. Jokes about German sausage are the wurst.

7. What happens if you eat yeast and shoe polish?

Every morning you'll rise and shine!

8. What kind of table can you eat?

A vege-table!

9. Why do hamburgers go to the gym?

To get better buns!

10. What is the difference between pizza puns and a pizza?

Pizza puns can't be topped!

11. Why does the girl hate French pancakes?

Because they give her the crepes!

12. Why was the chewing gum manufacturer arrested?

For unlicensed ex-spearmints!

13. Why was the salad full of rust?

Because it's a form of car-rot!

14. What is the only thing that can cure a sick do-nut?

An antidought!

15. What kind of music do coffee beans like?

Frappe music!

16. Why can't a burrito keep a secret?

They tend to spill the beans!

17. "I am going bananas!"

That's what I say to my bananas before I leave the house.

18. What is the most dangerous vegetable?

Bro killy!

19. What do you get if you cross a sweet potato and a jazz musician?

A yam session!

20. "This food tastes kind of funny."

"Then why aren't you laughing?"

21. What did the angry customer at the Italian restaurant give the chef?

A pizza of his mind!

22. Which is the left side of a pie?

The side that is not eaten!

23. A lot of people cry when they cut an onion.

The trick is not to form an emotional bond!

24. I went to a restaurant with a sign that said they served breakfast at any time.

So I ordered scrambled eggs during the Renaissance!

25. Did you hear about the cheese factory that exploded in France?

There was nothing left but de Brie!

26. What do you call leftover salad?

All that romaines!

Chapter Six
Mixed Jokes

1. What comes out of your nose at 150 mph?

Lambogreeny!

2. When is the worst time to open a window?

When you are on a submarine!

3. Do you have holes in your underwear?

Everyone does! Otherwise, you couldn't get them on!

4. Is your refrigerator running?

It's making headlines!

5. Which plant rules the garden?

The dande-lion!

6. I just read a book on reverse psychology.

Do not read it!

7. Why are obtuse angles so depressed?

Because they're never right!

8. Why should the number 2 8 8 never be mentioned?

It's two gross!

9. Why does the alphabet only have 25 letters?

I don't know Y!

10. Why did the man not like his sewing cushion?

He couldn't put a pin on it!

11. What is yellow and hurts when it is in your eye?

A steamroller!

12. A magician was walking down the street and turned into a grocery store.

13. I bought a new boomerang…

But I can't seem to throw the old one away!

14. What makes the calendar look so popular?

It has so many dates!

15. Why did the picture go to jail?

It was framed!

16. Shout out to anyone wondering what the opposite of in is.

17. I've just found the worst page in my dictionary.

The content is disgraceful, disgusting, dishonest, disingenuous, and disreputable.

18. Change is inevitable…

…except from a vending machine.

19. There are 3 kinds of people:

Those who can count and those who can't!

20. What do you call a dance for people who hate each other?

An avoidance!

21. Why is Peter Pan always flying?

He neverlands!

22. To make a mistake is human...

...but to blame it on someone else, now that's even more human.

23. How can you get four suits for a dollar?

Buy a deck of cards!

24. The 50-50-90 rule:

Anytime you have a 50/50 chance of getting something right, there's a 90% probability you'll get it wrong.

25. What's the difference between ignorance and apathy?

I don't know and I don't care!

26. I did a theatrical performance about puns.

It was a play on words!

27. Why is the grass so dangerous?

It's full of blades!

28. What did the tornado say to the sports car?

"Want to go for a spin?"

29. What do you call the little rivers that flow into the Nile?

Juve-Niles!

30. What kind of rocks are never found in the ocean?

Dry ones!

31. Why didn't the sun go to college?

Because it already had a million degrees!

32. What is the opposite of a cold front?

A warm back!

33. What is green, brown, and white, and can't climb a tree?

A fridge in a camo jacket!

34. What do you call a joke you tell while washing your hands?

A clean joke!

35. What do you call a paddle sale at the marina?

An oar deal!

36. Don't call me later.

You can just call me by my name!

37. What do you call a farm that grows bad jokes?

Corny!

38. What do you call a dead pine tree?

A nevergreen!

39. Did I tell you the time I fell in love during a backflip?

I was head-over-heels!

40. What do you call a factory that sells passable products?

A satisfactory!

41. I was doing okay until I covered my report card in butter...

Then my grades went downhill fast!

42. Want to hear a joke about a balloon?

Never mind, it got away from me!

43. What do you call a book that is about the brain?

A mind reader!

44 What do you call a country where everyone drives a red car?

A red carnation!

45. What is the difference between one yard and two yards?

A fence!

46. What happens when you see one shopping center?

You've seen the mall!

47. The past, the present, and the future walk into a room at the same time.

It was tense!

48. Why are rivers always rich?

Because they have two banks!

49. Why did the teapot take a break?

To blow off some steam!

50. The best time to open a gift is the present.

51. Why did the guy stack quarters on his head?

He wanted to change his mind!

52. Why shouldn't you spell 'part' backward?

Because it's a trap!

53. Why should you never try to eat a clock?

Because it's very time-consuming!

54. What did one aspiring wig say to the other aspiring wig?

I want to end up on top!

55. Change is hard.

Have you ever tried to bend a coin?

56. Not all math puns are bad.

Just sum!

57. My favorite color is purple.

I like it more than blue and red combined!

58. Why did the boy study on an airplane?

Because he wanted to get a higher education!

59. Why did the old lady go to jail?

Because she stole a kilt and plaid guilty!

60. The mattress thief was cot in the act, bed-handed.

61. How do you keep your dreams alive?

By hitting the snooze button!

62. Why are calendars so depressed?

Because their days are numbered!

63. What kind of jokes do towels tell?

Dry ones!

64. Did you pick your nose?

No, l was born with it!

65. What has a hundred heads and a hundred tails?

One hundred pennies!

66. What happened to the girl who ran away with the circus?

The police made her bring it back!

67. What did the shoes say to the hat?

"You go on a-head, l'll follow you on foot!"

68. Why did the house go to the doctor?

Because it had a window pane!

69. l used to have a fear of hurdles, but l got over it.

70. Why wouldn't the kid take a bath?

He said he didn't want to steal!

71. Why did the girl wear glasses during math class?

Because it improves di-vison!

72. Where can you always find money?

In the dictionary!

73. Daphne: "I wish I had enough money to buy a dinosaur."

Val: "What would you do with a dinosaur?"

Daphne: "Who wants a dinosaur? I just want the money!"

74. Why was the bad singer locked out of their house?

They couldn't find the right key!

75. What was stolen from the music store?

The lute!

76. What is big, scary, and has three wheels?

A monster riding a tricycle!

77. What type of lightning likes to play sports?

Ball lightning!

78. What is the hardest part about skydiving?

The ground!

79. Do you go rock climbing?

I would if I were boulder!

80. What is the shortest month?

May, because it has only three letters!

81. I was going to look for my missing watch, but I could never find the time.

82. Where was the Declaration of Independence signed?

At the bottom!

83. Have I told you this déjà vu joke before?

84. What does a houseboat turn into when it grows up?

A township!

85. No matter how cold you get, never build a fire in a kayak!

You can't have your kayak and heat it too!

86. What do you find in the middle of nowhere?

The letter "h"!

87. What should you take on a trip to the desert?

A thirst-aid kit!

88. What always comes at the beginning of parades?

The letter "p"!

89. I thought I'd tell you a brilliant time-travel joke...

But you didn't like it!

90. What kind of match is hard to get out of the box?

A wrestling match!

91. What is the best time to travel to the sun?

At night!

92. When I was born, I was so surprised I didn't talk for a year and a half.

93. What is on the Earth all the time, but never gets dirty?

Your shadow!

94. When I'm up, it's lying down.

When I'm lying, it's up.

What is it?

My foot!

95. What runs but never walks?

A hose!

96. Why is 1+1=3 like your left foot?

It's not right!

97. Why did the book join the police force?

He wanted to go undercover!

98. What did the student say when his teacher asked him to use geometry in a sentence?

"A little acorn grew and grew until it finally awoke one day and said, 'Gee, I'm a tree.'"

99. I don't play soccer because I enjoy the sport.

I'm just doing it for kicks.

100. What has no fingers, but many rings?

A tree!

101. I used to work in a shoe recycling shop.

It was sole destroying!

102. Is this pool safe for diving?

It deep ends!

103. What is SCHOOL an acronym for?

Seven Crappy Hours Of Our Life

104. What is the highest form of flattery?

A plateau!

105. There is no "l" in Denial.

106. What is the cheapest diamond you can buy?

A pack of playing cards!

107. "Why did you walk away while we were talking?"

"You were boring me to death, and my survival instinct kicked in."

Conclusion

If you just didn't get enough laughs, then color us surprised! Still, we haven't turned away an audience yet! We have tons of jokes for all ages, and even more on the way, in our whole series of *You Laugh You Lose* books! Make sure to check back frequently with our growing library of riddle and joke books. Fun for the whole family, and all your friends too!

www.ingramcontent.com/pod-product-compliance
Lightning Source LLC
Chambersburg PA
CBHW052239150726
48002CB00003B/1502